D1203446

Georgia, My State
Native Americans

Georgia's First People

Book 1

by Jill Ward

STATE
STANDARDS
PUBLISHING

Your State • Your Standards • Your Grade Level

Dear Educators, Librarians and Parents ...

Thank you for choosing the *"Georgia, My State"* Series! We have designed this series to support the Georgia Department of Education's Georgia Performance Standards for elementary level Georgia studies. Each book in the series has been written at appropriate grade level as measured by the ATOS Readability Formula for Books (Accelerated Reader), the Lexile Framework for Reading, and the Fountas & Pinnell Benchmark Assessment System for Guided Reading. Photographs and/or illustrations, captions, and other design elements have been included to provide supportive visual messaging to enhance text comprehension. Glossary and Word Index sections introduce key new words and help young readers develop skills in locating and combining information.

We wish you all success in using the *"Georgia, My State"* Series to meet your student or child's learning needs. For additional sources of information, see www.georgiaencyclopedia.org.

Jill Ward, President

Publisher
State Standards Publishing, LLC
1788 Quail Hollow
Hamilton, GA 31811
USA
1.866.740.3056
www.statestandardspublishing.com

Library of Congress Cataloging-in-Publication Data
Ward, Jill, 1952-
   Georgia's first people / by Jill Ward.
      p. cm. -- (Georgia, my state. Native Americans ; book 1)
   ISBN-13: 978-1-935077-74-9 (hardcover)
   ISBN-10: 1-935077-74-0 (hardcover)
   ISBN-13: 978-1-935077-81-7 (pbk.)
   ISBN-10: 1-935077-81-3 (pbk.)
   1. Paleo-Indians--Georgia--Juvenile literature. 2. Georgia--Antiquities--Juvenile literature.
I. Title.
   E78.G3W27 2010
   970.01--dc22
                                        2010005900

Printed in the United States of America, North Mankato, Minnesota, March 2010, 120209.

About the Author

Jill Ward has more than twenty years' experience as a creative writer for business and organization promotional and educational needs, including video scripts, brochures, marketing and educational materials, white papers, and feature articles. She is the founder and president of State Standards Publishing and lives in Georgia with her husband, Harry.

Table of Contents

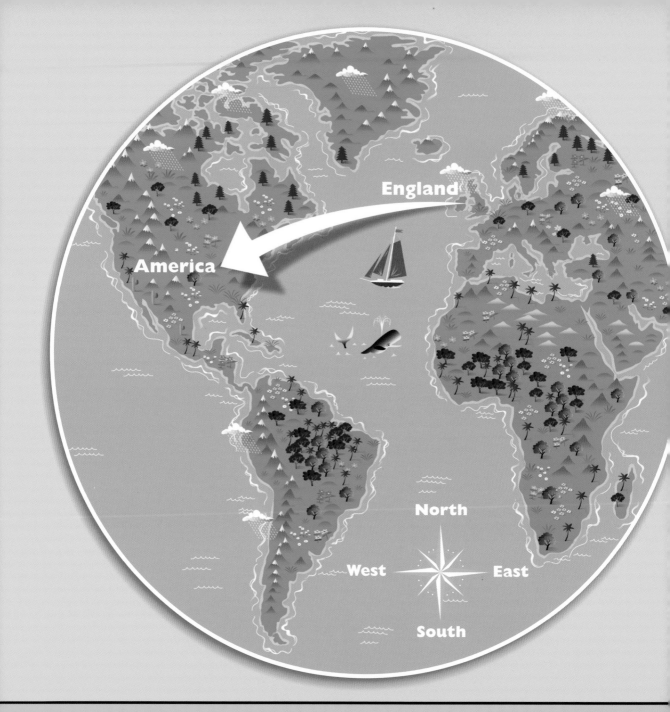

People from England came to America. They started colonies.

First People

In the 1500s, people from England began coming to America. They started **colonies**. They made new homes in a new land. These colonies one day became states, like Georgia.

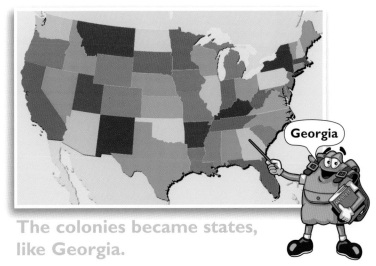

The colonies became states, like Georgia.

Native Americans were the first type of people to live in America.

But long before the 1500s, **Native Americans** lived on the land. They were **native** to America. They were the first type of people to live in America. Native Americans are sometimes called **Indians**.

The first Native Americans were Paleo-Indians.

Thousands of Years Ago!

The first Native Americans lived here thousands of years ago! That's a very long time! These people are called Paleo-Indians. **Paleo** means ancient, or very old. It also means **prehistoric**. This is the time before people started writing down our history.

Siberia

Dry Ground

Alaska

Canada

United States of America

North

West   East

South

The Paleo-Indians may have walked from Siberia to Alaska.

Coming to America

Scientists believe that the Paleo-Indians came from a country called Siberia. This is near the state of Alaska. Today, there is water between Siberia and Alaska. But then, the ground was dry. The people may have walked to Alaska.

Today, there is water between Siberia and Alaska.

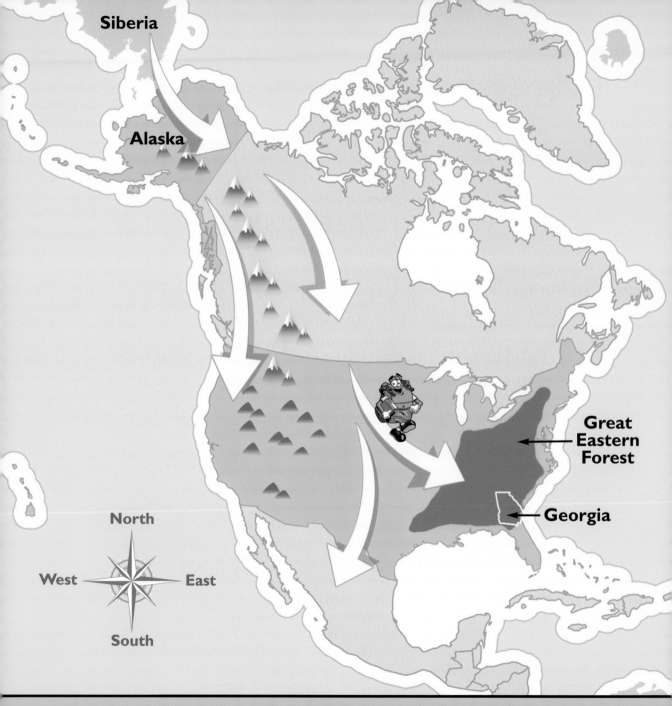

Siberia

Alaska

Great
Eastern
Forest

Georgia

North

West ✦ East

South

The Paleo-Indians spread out across America.

Groups of Paleo-Indians spread out across America. Some came to Georgia. They learned to live in the **Great Eastern Forest**. The forest covered the eastern part of America. It covered Georgia, too.

Paleo-Indians lived in small groups of families called bands.

Moving in Bands

Paleo-Indians had to travel to find food. They did not stay in one place very long. They wandered. They lived in small groups of families called **bands**. Bands were usually made of brothers and their wives and children.

Paleo-Indian men hunted wild animals with spears.

Hunting with Spears

Paleo-Indian men hunted wild animals with **spears**. Their spears were wooden sticks with a sharp point. The points were made of rock like **flint** or **quartz**. The hunters chipped the rock to make it sharp.

Hunters chipped the rock to make it sharp.

Women and children gathered food.

Gathering Food

Women and children gathered food.

The people ate nuts, berries, and fruits.

They also ate roots, seeds, and tree

bark. The people made small shelters

out of bones and sticks covered with

animal skins. They

made clothes from

animal skins, too.

The people made shelters out of sticks and animal skins.

Paleo-Indian Artifacts Have Been Found Near These Places in Georgia.

Appalachian Plateau

Blue Ridge Mountains

Valley and Ridge

Piedmont

Upper Coastal Plain

Lower Coastal Plain

MY STATE

1. Lake Allatoona
2. Greensboro
3. Augusta
4. Macon
5. Brier Creek
6. Albany
7. Douglas

Artifacts Tell Us About Them

Scientists have found Paleo-Indian **artifacts** in some places in Georgia. Artifacts are things made by people. Spear points and other Indian tools are artifacts. They tell us about the people who once lived here.

Artifacts tell us about the people who once lived here.

Glossary

artifacts – Things made by people that tell us something about them. Spear points and other Indian tools are artifacts.

bands – Small groups of Paleo-Indians. Bands were usually made of brothers and their wives and children.

colonies – Places where groups of people make new homes in a new land.

flint – A type of rock used for making spear points.

Great Eastern Forest – A forest that covered the eastern part of America.

Indians – Another name for Native Americans.

native – The first type of people to live in a place.

Native Americans – The first type of people to live in America.

paleo – Ancient, or very old.

prehistoric – The time before people started writing down history.

quartz – A type of rock used for making spear points.

spears – Wood sticks with a sharp point made of rock. Spears are used for hunting.

Word Index

Image Credits

Cover   "American Indian Life in the Paleo-Indian Period" painting by Susan A. Walton, © Susan A. Walton, Ohio Historical Society
p. 4   Globe map: © John Woodcock, iStockphoto.com
p. 5   US map: © John Woodcock, iStockphoto.com
p. 6   Native Americans: © HultonArchive, iStockphoto.com
p. 8   "American Indian Life in the Paleo-Indian Period" painting by Susan A. Walton, © Susan A. Walton, Ohio Historical Society
p. 10   Map: © Edward Grajeda, iStockphoto.com
p. 11   Map: © Edward Grajeda, iStockphoto.com
p. 12   Map: © Edward Grajeda, iStockphoto.com
p. 14   "Indian Band" painting by Greg Harlin, © Frank H. McClung Museum, The University of Tennessee, Knoxville
p. 16   Hunter: © Marilyn Angel Wynn, NativeStock.com
p. 17   Spear point: © Brian Brockman, iStockphoto.com
p. 18   Woman gathering: © Marilyn Angel Wynn, NativeStock.com
p. 19   Dwelling: © Marilyn Angel Wynn, NativeStock.com
p. 21   Artifacts: © Marilyn Angel Wynn, NativeStock.com
p. 24   Woodland Indian: © Buddy Mays, Travel Stock Photography, buddymays.com; All other images: © Marilyn Angel Wynn, NativeStock.com

Editorial Credits

Designer: Michael Sellner, Corporate Graphics, North Mankato, Minnesota

Native Americans Time Line

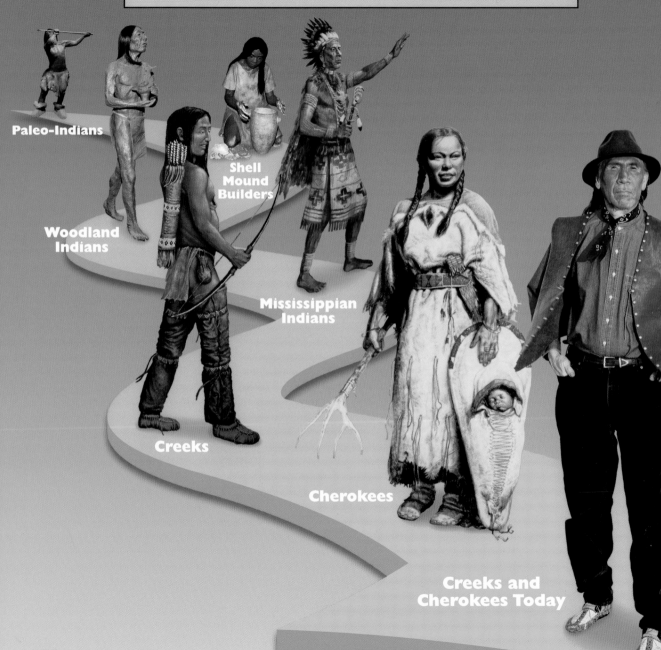

Paleo-Indians

Woodland Indians

Shell Mound Builders

Mississippian Indians

Creeks

Cherokees

Creeks and Cherokees Today